I0413506

About the Marine Sanctuaries Conservation Series

The National Oceanic and Atmospheric Administration's Office of National Marine Sanctuaries (ONMS) administers the National Marine Sanctuary Program. Its mission is to identify, designate, protect and manage the ecological, recreational, research, educational, historical, and aesthetic resources and qualities of nationally significant coastal and marine areas. The existing marine sanctuaries differ widely in their natural and historical resources and include nearshore and open ocean areas ranging in size from less than one to over 5,000 square miles. Protected habitats include rocky coasts, kelp forests, coral reefs, sea grass beds, estuarine habitats, hard and soft bottom habitats, segments of whale migration routes, and shipwrecks.

Because of considerable differences in settings, resources, and threats, each marine sanctuary has a tailored management plan. Conservation, education, research, monitoring and enforcement programs vary accordingly. The integration of these programs is fundamental to marine protected area management. The Marine Sanctuaries Conservation Series reflects and supports this integration by providing a forum for publication and discussion of the complex issues currently facing the National Marine Sanctuary Program. Topics of published reports vary substantially and may include descriptions of educational programs, discussions on resource management issues, and results of scientific research and monitoring projects. The series facilitates integration of natural sciences, socioeconomic and cultural sciences, education, and policy development to accomplish the diverse needs of NOAA's resource protection mandate.

Conservation Science
in NOAA's National Marine Sanctuaries:
Description and Recent Accomplishments

Compiler: Stephen R. Gittings

National Oceanic and Atmospheric Administration
National Marine Sanctuary Program

U.S. Department of Commerce
Carlos M. Gutierrez, Secretary

National Oceanic and Atmospheric Administration
VADM Conrad C. Lautenbacher, Jr. (USN-ret.)
Under Secretary of Commerce for Oceans and Atmosphere

National Ocean Service
John H. Dunnigan, Assistant Administrator

Silver Spring, Maryland
June 2006

Office of National Marine Sanctuaries
Daniel J. Basta, Director

DISCLAIMER

Report content does not necessarily reflect the views and policies of the Office of National Marine Sanctuaries or the National Oceanic and Atmospheric Administration, nor does the mention of trade names or commercial products constitute endorsement or recommendation for use.

REPORT AVAILABILITY

Electronic copies of this report may be downloaded from the National Marine Sanctuaries Program web site at www.sanctuaries.nos.noaa.gov. Hard copies may be available from the following address:

> National Oceanic and Atmospheric Administration
> Office of National Marine Sanctuaries
> SSMC4, N/ORM62
> 1305 East-West Highway
> Silver Spring, MD 20910

COVER

Clockwise from left: Whale concentrations and vessel traffic separation scheme – David Wiley, Michael Thompson, Richard Merrick, NOAA; Lobster size and abundance – Florida Fish and Wildlife Conservation Commission, Fish and Wildlife Research Institute; Net sampling from the NOAA Ship *David Starr Jordan* - Cordell Bank NMS

SUGGESTED CITATION

Gittings, Stephen R. 2006. Conservation Science in NOAA's National Marine Sanctuaries: Description and Recent Accomplishments. Marine Sanctuaries Conservation Series ONMS-06-04. U.S. Department of Commerce, National Oceanic and Atmospheric Administration, Office of National Marine Sanctuaries, Silver Spring, MD. 30 pp.

CONTACT

Stephen R. Gittings, Science Program Manager
NOAA National Marine Sanctuary Program
1305 East West Highway, N/ORM62
Silver Spring, MD 20910
steve.gittings@noaa.gov

ABSTRACT

This report describes cases relating to the management of national marine sanctuaries in which certain scientific information was required so managers could make decisions that effectively protected trust resources. The cases presented represent only a fraction of difficult issues that marine sanctuary managers deal with daily. They include, among others, problems related to wildlife disturbance, vessel routing, marine reserve placement, watershed management, oil spill response, and habitat restoration. Scientific approaches to address these problems vary significantly, and include literature surveys, data mining, field studies (monitoring, mapping, observations, and measurement), geospatial and biogeographic analysis, and modeling. In most cases there is also an element of expert consultation and collaboration among multiple partners, agencies with resource protection responsibilities, and other users and stakeholders. The resulting management responses may involve direct intervention (e.g., for spill response or habitat restoration issues), proposal of boundary alternatives for marine sanctuaries or reserves, changes in agency policy or regulations, making recommendations to other agencies with resource protection responsibilities, proposing changes to international or domestic shipping rules, or development of new education or outreach programs.

KEY WORDS

Conservation science, national marine sanctuaries, resource management, marine reserves, biogeography, watersheds, emergency response, seagrass restoration, dispersants, wildlife disturbance, marine mammals, seamounts, database management, vessel routing, deep coral

TABLE OF CONTENTS

INTRODUCTION

The National Oceanic and Atmospheric Administration depends heavily on the applied sciences to accomplish virtually all major components of it missions, most of which contribute significantly to the U.S. economy. For example, weather prediction capabilities continue to improve, as do scientific and technological advances that improve navigational safety. Studies of ocean dynamics promote better understanding of the impacts of changes in climate and weather, the vulnerabilities of coastal communities to sea level changes, environmental controls on marine fisheries and protected species, and the most efficient responses to oil spills and chemical pollution. And with so much attention focused on such critical issues as national security and disaster relief, it is more important than ever to use budget resources wisely. For NOAA, this means applying the best available information to issues of national importance and focusing scientific efforts to address critical knowledge gaps for these issues.

NOAA's National Marine Sanctuary Program (NMSP, http://www.sanctuaries.noaa.gov/) serves as the trustee for a system of 13 underwater parks, encompassing more than 18,000 square miles of marine and Great Lakes waters from Washington State to the Florida Keys, and from Lake Huron to American Samoa. The NMSP employs a conservation science approach to conduct, sponsor, and facilitate research that is fundamental to understanding the nature and uses of natural and cultural resources in marine sanctuaries. The NMSP defines conservation science as "*areas of scientific investigation concerned with the preservation of natural and cultural resources.*" For the NMSP, this includes activities related to characterization, monitoring, and research focused on improved understanding, assessment, evaluation, protection, and restoration of its trust resources. The mission-directed approach of conservation science allows sanctuary staff and many partners to document the condition and trends of these protected ecosystems as well as the significance of emerging threats, and to develop assessment and response capabilities that ensure effective management. The Program evaluates management practices, provides improved understanding for future management decisions, and strengthens

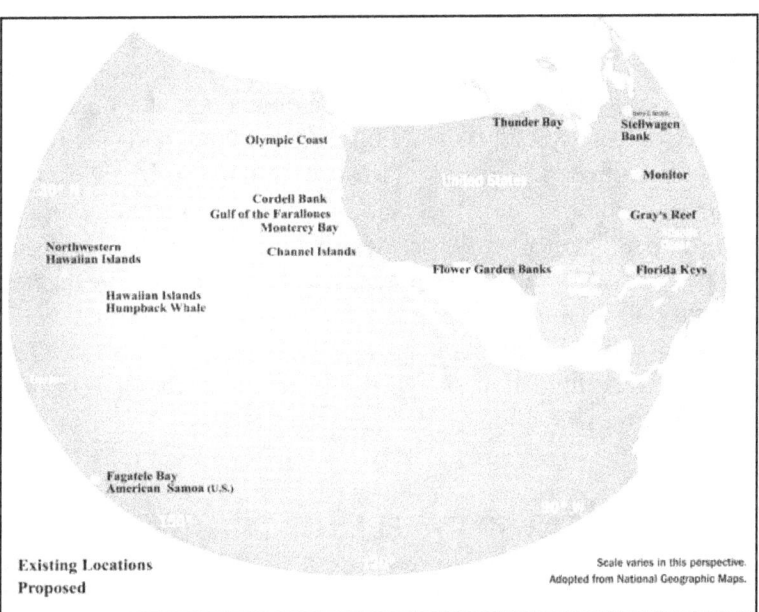

In 1972, exactly one hundred years after the first national park was created, the nation made a similar commitment to preserving its marine treasures by establishing the National Marine Sanctuary Program. Since then, thirteen national marine sanctuaries, representing a wide variety of ocean environments, have been designated.

the role of the NMSP in supporting broader, NOAA-wide responsibilities for coastal management.

Conservation science in the marine sanctuaries involves coordination between national and local sanctuary programs, between the NMSP and regional and national science support agencies, and between sanctuaries and their local support networks. Priorities are determined based on input at all levels and are issues of national and local importance. Annual operating plans for the sanctuaries provide the approach to setting priorities, and partnerships at all levels provide the mechanism for funding and other science support. In all cases, science programs are driven by management needs and related performance measures, and evaluated accordingly.

SCIENCE OPERATIONS IN THE NMSP

The National Programs Branch of the NMSP coordinates a Science Council consisting of headquarters and regional representatives, and site Research Coordinators implement conservation science initiatives related to planning, site-based monitoring, site characterizations, and targeted scientific research. A Science Plan, as well as science needs documents and a framework for system-wide monitoring provide guidance for establishing the program's scientific foundation, enable it to accomplish priority tasks, and contribute to the annual planning process for the sites and the national program. The Science Plan stresses the need for effective programs of site assessment, research and resource monitoring at local, regional and national levels to identify information needs, track emerging threats, manage risks, and provide input to inform policy. In addition, it is integrated with NMSP education and outreach efforts. Feedback from these functional elements, in turn, bears on annual and longer-term science priorities and efforts. In combination, the NMSP can address the diverse needs of its broad resource protection mandate.

OPERATING PRINCIPLES OF THE CONSERVATION SCIENCE PROGRAM

- Site assessment and characterization data allow managers to better understand the protected natural and cultural resources and important environmental processes and threats in the NMSs. This enables effective policy development, risk management, and threat reduction as well as enhance education and outreach programs of the NMSs.

- Monitoring data are acquired and compiled, allowing managers to establish baseline conditions and discern trends including changes in resources caused by management actions so they may effectively conserve, enhance, and restore habitats and ecosystems, as well as contribute to larger-scale ocean observing systems.

- Research results demonstrate linkages between nature and human activities, and contribute to effective resource management by facilitating information-based decision-making.

SCIENCE PRIORITIES

Priority issues are identified each spring in discussions involving sanctuary managers, research coordinators, and national program staff. Annual priorities not only provide direction for research efforts, but also establish the framework for annual operating plans, which in turn affect budget planning. Two examples of current priority conservation science areas include the implementation of a system-wide approach to resource monitoring and a focus on sanctuary site characterizations. As an example of how this affects sanctuary operations, design approaches established for sanctuary monitoring were recently applied to the development of a plan for assessing the effectiveness of marine reserves in the Channel Islands NMS. The results of these evaluations will be critical to decisions about location and sizing of future reserves and in modifying existing reserves to better protect and restore ecosystems. Our efforts to produce comprehensive characterizations for all sanctuaries will result in tools that will guide management, inform the public, and meet performance measures and Congressional requirements for adequate characterizations throughout the NMSP.

Most sanctuaries develop annual research plans that address site-specific and national research priorities. Some do so in cooperation with informal or formal advisory groups. For example, Monterey Bay NMS has a Research Activities Panel that convenes regularly to discuss issues related to research in the sanctuary and assists the site in development of its plans. Smaller sites, like the Flower Garden Banks NMS, have informal groups of advisors that may not meet, but are called on to review and comment on various plans and reports, and may provide recommendations to the sites. In other cases, like the Olympic Coast NMS, annual information transfer and planning meetings may be held. In addition to enhancing communication between investigators working in sanctuaries, these meetings allow the sites to compile research reports, stimulate interest in sanctuary research, obtain input on priority research areas, convey management-related research needs to the scientific community, and plan for future years.

SCIENCE FUNDING AND COLLABORATION

Some funding for research programs comes from individual sanctuary budgets, but the majority of funding comes from other NOAA line offices (e.g., the National Centers for Coastal Ocean Science) and programs (e.g., Coral Reef Conservation Program), other governmental agencies and the private sector. Generally speaking, very little research, either intramural or extramural, is funded directly from sanctuary budgets. In FY05, NMSP funds for research and monitoring totaled $4.7M at all sanctuaries (12% of the Program budget).

Considerable effort is focused on facilitating research in sanctuaries through offers of logistical support, including free use of sanctuary boats and field stations, and arranging for time aboard NOAA ships. The sites, as well as national staff, also work with other agencies to provide incentive for investigators proposing work in sanctuaries. For example, the scientific guidance distributed annually to the regional centers funded by NOAA's National Undersea Research Program contains discussions of the research priorities of NMSP. In addition, NMSP program staff are working with the U.S. Geological Survey to enhance USGS efforts related to site characterizations in the sanctuaries. Private sector partnerships are developed at both the local and national levels. For example, several oil companies have actively supported research at the Flower Garden Banks NMS through donations to a non-profit support organization called the Flower Gardens Fund (part of the Gulf of Mexico Foundation). At the national level, a five-year partnership with National Geographic resulted in the high profile Sustainable Seas Expeditions. Environmental Systems Research, Inc. (ESRI) donated comprehensive GIS software packages to each site to enhance the Protected Area GIS (PAGIS) initiative. Non-profit organizations also support sanctuary research. The Monterey Bay Aquarium Research Institute conducts considerable research in that region. The Reef Environmental Education Foundation (REEF) conducts fish censuses in almost all sanctuaries, providing data for site characterizations, monitoring, and specific issues such as zone effectiveness.

Scientific results are disseminated in numerous ways, depending on their content, level of specificity, and potential application. Some are used to generate internal management-support products through GIS databases (primarily integrated maps), time-series graphics, and predictive models. Many prepared reports are reviewed and published in the Marine Sanctuaries Conservation Series, a periodic technical report of the NMSP, or technical journals of partner organizations. These reports, like most information published by the Program, are available in print and on the organization websites. In some cases, project data are also available from partner websites. For example, fish census data can be obtained from the REEF website and reports can be prepared interactively for any region of the country. Many research projects result in publication in peer-reviewed scientific journals. In some cases, journals have prepared special issues on sanctuary science (e.g. Gulf of Mexico Science, Marine Technology Society Journal).

Sanctuary websites are rich sources of data and information on NMSP science. Monterey Bay NMS, with funds from the David and Lucile Packard Foundation and the support of its many research partners, developed a particularly impressive website as part of the Sanctuary Integrated Monitoring Network (SIMoN, http://www.mbnms-simon.org/). It provides extensive information about past and on-going projects and results, has interactive mapping capabilities and in-depth descriptions of sanctuary resources, and provides appropriate links to sources of additional information or data. The NMSP is working to expand the capabilities of SIMoN to marine sanctuaries throughout the country.

NMSP CONSERVATION SCIENCE IN ACTION

On the following pages are individual examples of management issues that have been addressed using various types of information derived from scientific observations and investigations in marine sanctuaries. They represent, of course, only a fraction of the issues that a marine sanctuary manager must face, but they illustrate a range of management issues, scientific approaches, and products required by managers to make informed decisions about activities and policies necessary to protect sanctuary resources. They also illustrate the variety of partners participating in sanctuary science and resource management, the variety of decision tools available, and the many response alternatives available.

In many cases, the scientific information used to support a management action is obtained and made available to the NMSP by scientists from other Federal or State agencies, or academic institutions and not by staff scientists. Furthermore, the ultimate management action is often implemented by another resource management entity, but in consultation with NMSP staff and in the interest of protecting sanctuary resources. So while these examples represent only a subset of issues addressed by sanctuary managers, they provide a glimpse into the highly collaborative and cooperative approach used to meet the resource protection responsibilities of the National Marine Sanctuary Program.

Channel Islands National Marine Sanctuary

Management Issue

Advancing the Science and Policy of Marine Reserves

The Channel Islands National Marine Sanctuary (Sanctuary) and the State of California (State) sponsored a four year community-based process, supported by a Science Advisory Panel (SAP), to address a long-term decline in the health of the Channel Islands marine ecosystem. The local community recommended marine reserves (no-take zones) as one solution to protect and restore natural habitats and living resources and to provide undisturbed reference areas for ecosystem-based research and education. The best available ecological and socio-economic data were applied to design and evaluate marine reserve network options. Spatial modeling supported the scientific and community evaluation of options.

Information Needs

- Habitat type and distribution data (e.g. kelp forest, rocky reef, coastline, emergent rocks)
- Spatial data on consumptive (e.g. commercial and sport fishing) and non-consumptive (e.g. recreational diving) uses
- Fish, invertebrate, algae, marine mammal, and seabird life history data

Scientific Approach and Actions

- The SAP, representing multiple disciplines, agencies and institutions, developed ecological criteria for marine reserve design and evaluation

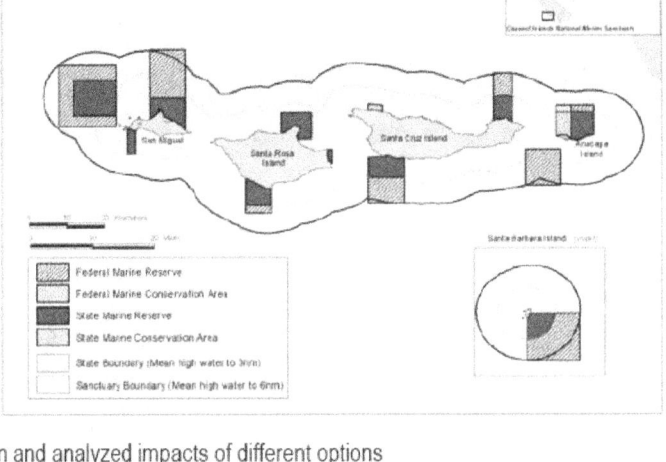

- Team of NOAA socio-economists collected spatially explicit user information and analyzed impacts of different options
- Application of SPEXAN, a modeling program, to identify conservation "hot spots" and evaluate design options.
- Development of the Channel Islands Spatial Support and Analysis Tool, a geospatial modeling tool that stakeholders used to visualize, query and apply ecological and socio-economic data to generate marine reserve network options

Key Partners and Information Sources

California Department of Fish and Game, NOAA National Marine Fisheries Service, NOAA Coastal Services Center, US Geological Survey, Channel Islands National Park, University of California Santa Barbara's Marine Science Institute, Partnership for Interdisciplinary Studies of Coastal Oceans, Pfleger Institute of Environmental Research, Sanctuary Advisory Council and Marine Reserves Working Group

Results and Decision Support Products

- GIS Database containing Sanctuary habitat, living marine resource and human use data
- Channel Islands Spatial Support and Analysis Tool
- Ecological criteria for reserve design and impact analysis
- Socioeconomic baseline information for impact analysis and monitoring

Management Response

- In 2003, the State established a network of 10 marine reserves and two marine conservation areas, including 100 sq. nautical miles of nearshore habitats in the Sanctuary. This is the largest network of marine reserves along the west coast of the United States.
- The Sanctuary may extend the network into deeper waters to capture the full suite of Sanctuary habitats
- The State and Sanctuary developed biological and socio-economic monitoring plans to evaluate the effectiveness of the network; established cooperative enforcement protocols with the U.S. Coast Guard and National Park Service; produced brochures, signage and presentations to inform commercial and recreational users and the general public.

Channel Islands National Marine Sanctuary

Management Issue

Emergency Response

Channel Islands NMS is a designated first responder for the region within and around the Sanctuary. The CINMS Lake Seawolf aircraft is used for initial reconnaissance and mapping missions after incidents such as oil spills and vessel groundings. The CINMS also uses two vessel platforms, a 28' Wilson fast response boat, and R/V Shearwater, a 62' catameran research vessel to carry response personnel to an incident for on water surveys, SCUBA surveys, and pollution testing and sampling. CINMS staff are trained in Hazardous Waste Prevention and Emergency Response, Shoreline Cleanup and Assesment Training, Offshore Hazardous Environment Operations, Geographic Information Systems (GIS), Global Positioning Systems (GPS), and Remote Sensing.

Information Needs
- Physical features: bathymetry; topography; shorelines; geology.
- Biological features: habitats; flora and fauna species distributions; key and endangered species.
- Oceanographic: surface and subsurface currents; tides; sea surface temperatures.
- Socioeconomic: historic shipwrecks, sensitive cultural resources, commercial and recreational use areas.

Scientific Approach and Actions
- Aerial Mapping: Aerial surveys are recorded in the Sanctuary Aerial Monitoring and Spatial Analysis Program (SAMSAP) in real-time. GIS maps of conditions, affected resources, slick extent, and slick migration projections are created and distributed to responders.
- NOAA buoy and satellite data are used and combined with GIS maps to create imagery and remotely sensed analyses of current and projected conditions that affect response.

Key Partners and Information Sources

NOAA agencies: HAZMAT, National Data Buoy Center, Coastwatch, National Environmental Satellite Data & Information Service, & National Weather Service; Other agencies: US Coast Guard, US Navy, National Park Service, California Department of Fish & Game Office of Spill Prevention & Response, Minerals Management Service.

Decision Support Products
- Sanctuary Aerial Monitoring and Spatial Analysis Program software
- Maps (physical, biological, socioeconomic); remotely sensed imagery; resources at risk; ocean current profiles; priority response areas; risk migration; long term analysis.

Management Response
➢ Fast response capability with two vessels and an aircraft; portable GIS/GPS survey software (SAMSAP) with multi-platform capability; full GIS / Remote Sensing analysis capability; trained response personnel; "grab and go" emergency response packs with data recording equipment (e.g., GPS units) and sample collection equipment.; 24 hour emergency pager.
➢ Alaska Airlines Flight 261 crash response: CINMS provided initial and ongoing scientific support to the emergency response during search and rescue and salvage and recovery efforts in response to the crash. CINMS staff provided initial bathymetry maps, seafloor obstruction data, Remotely Operated Vehicle imagery and debris tracking data. CINMS personnel worked in aerial and on-water survey crews.
➢ Vessel groundings and oil spills: CINMS provides the US Coast Guard with aerial reconnaissance of vessel groundings and oil spills, photographing and mapping damage, leaking fuels, and resources at risk. Using oceanographic data provided by NOAA technology (buoys, satellites, etc.), staff create GIS products to monitor and track state of resources before, during, and after the event. CINMS also conducts site damage assessments on water, via SCUBA, and on the shoreline.

Channel Islands National Marine Sanctuary

Management Issue:

Evaluate Boundary Alternatives through Biogeographic Assessment

Channel Islands NMS was designated in 1980 and encompasses a large area of rocky coastline, kelp beds, and sea floor located off the coast of southern California. The islands and surrounding waters were selected as a Sanctuary due to their unique geological formations, natural resources, and cultural significance. At the time of Sanctuary designation, its boundaries extended from mean high tide offshore to a distance of six nautical miles. This area was selected to provide adequate protection of the resource given the limited information on the spatial distribution of threats, uses, biota, and habitats that was available at the time. NOAA's National Marine Sanctuary Program (NMSP) and CINMS are currently considering six alternatives for adjusting Sanctuary boundaries. Identifying how the six options overlay with the distribution of biotic and habitat resources is a critical component of assessing their effectiveness for meeting sanctuary objectives.

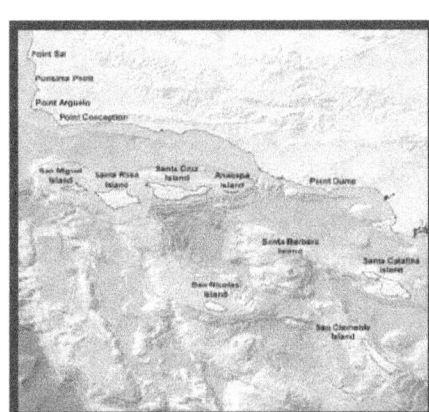

Information Needs

- Data compilation to identify spatially important areas for species and communities
- Analysis of the existing data for patterns or trends in the distribution of marine associated fauna
- Modeling the distribution of selected species in areas with insufficient data to ascertain likely distributions
- Using patterns and trends to understand the biogeography of the region in general
- Determine how these patterns and trends relate to proposed Sanctuary boundary alternatives

Scientific Approach and Actions

- Gather existing spatial biological and environmental data
- Evaluate data extent, quality, and position relative to alternative boundary options
- Produce modeling, data integration, and quantitative assessment of biotic and habitat resources for each boundary scenario

Key Partners and Information Sources

National Centers for Coastal Ocean Science, Center for Coastal Monitoring and Assessment, Channel Islands National Marine Sanctuary, Office of National Marine Sanctuaries, University of California, Santa Barbara, and Southern California Coastal Water Research Project Authority (SCCWRP)

Results and Decision Support Products

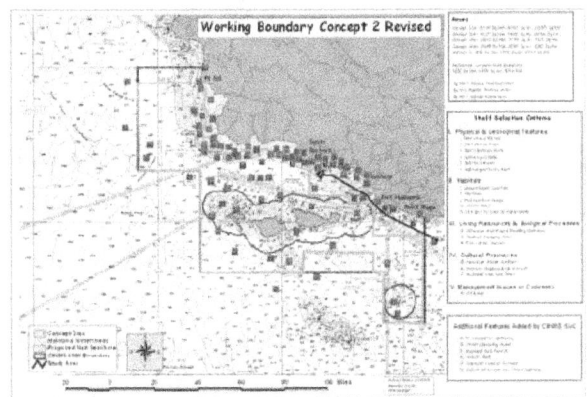

- Technical report on the biogeographic assessment of CINMS and surrounding waters
- Rank of proposed boundary concepts to favor areas of high primary productivity that are typically associated with high species richness and diversity.

Management Response

The sanctuary is informing stakeholder communities about the utility and availability of these products. The results of the assessments are being incorporated into a CINMS Supplemental EIS. The products will also be used to support science and education, and to inform other spatially explicit management decisions.

For more information: NCCOS. 2005. A biogeographic assessment of the Channel Islands National Marine Sanctuary: A review of boundary expansion concepts for NOAA's National Marine Sanctuary Program. NOAA Tech. Memorandum NOS NCCOS 21, 215 pp. Additional information can be found at: http://ccma.nos.noaa.gov/products/biogeography/cinms/report.html

Channel Islands National Marine Sanctuary

Management Issue

Evaluating Potential Displacement of a Network of Marine Reserves

The Sanctuary Aerial Monitoring and Spatial Analysis Program (SAMSAP) is designed to monitor and analyze physical and anthropogenic phenomena within the Channel Islands National Marine Sanctuary. Aerial surveys of the sanctuary are conducted as weather conditions allow, in a Lake Amphibian aircraft. A GPS collection strategy used onboard the aircraft allows real time data collection vital to management and resource protection. The information is used to monitor kelp distribution, marine mammal populations and migration patterns, and general ecosystem health within the sanctuary. Surveys of vessel traffic and vessel type allow historic and current anthropogenic use patterns to be studied.

The sanctuary recently used data collected by SAMSAP to examine the socioeconomic impacts that could result from an extension of the existing state network of marine protected areas (MPAs) into federal, deeper waters. The analysis of vessel observations between 1997 and 2004 evaluates potential displacement of fishing effort for a suite of spatial alternatives. The results are included as part of a comprehensive environmental impact statement.

Scientific Approach

- Vessel observations were delineated from other observed phenomena and converted into a GIS layer.
- The impact analysis was conducted within a GIS, which included vessel observations within the sanctuary and the two alternatives.
- The distribution of vessels within the two alternatives was quantified.

Results

- The greatest vessel activity occurred in the sanctuary's state waters, where no new MPAs are proposed. Over 91% of the 7,094 observed vessels were located in State waters.
- 15.1% of observed vessels occurred in the existing state MPA network.
- A small proportion of observed vessels were located in the additional, deeper waters proposed in the two alternatives. The preferred alternative contained 1% of all vessel observations, while Alternative 1 contained 2% of all observations.

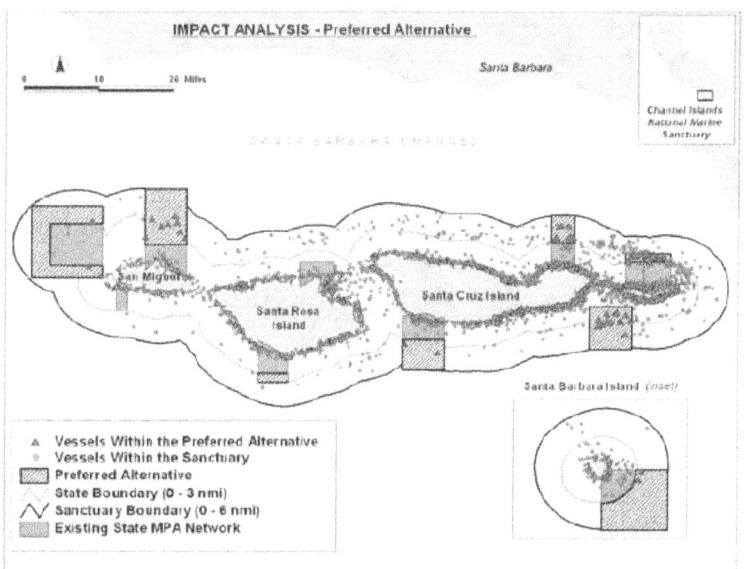

Management Response

- The SAMSAP analysis concluded that little vessel activity occurs in the Sanctuary's deeper, federal waters, indicating that neither alternative would likely result in a significant, negative impact on consumptive activities.
- SAMSAP was instrumental in forecasting and characterizing any potential displacement of fishing effort and will continue to be used to monitor sanctuary use and resource status.

Fagatele Bay National Marine Sanctuary

Management Issue

Are Watersheds Driving Change and Recovery on American Samoa's Coral Reefs?

The coral reefs of Fagatele Bay National Marine Sanctuary and American Samoa have shown steady recovery from coral damage caused by cyclones, predation by crown-of-thorns starfish outbreaks, and blast fishing that have occurred over the last 25 years. However, this recovery has been uneven around the island of Tutuila, where the Sanctuary is located. In addition, the size of fish and their numbers have not paralleled the increases in the benthic communities. Resource managers in American Samoa debate whether the recovery of fish populations is limited by land-derived stresses or by fishing pressure. Fagatele Bay NMS is an important tool for investigating this issue.

Information Needs

The extent to which watersheds are influencing fish and coral populations around Tutuila Island and within the Sanctuary; ranking of watersheds based on criteria that may influence coastal conditions, combined with a quantitative assessment of adjacent coral reef ecosystem conditions.

Scientific Approach and Actions

No single agency or research effort in American Samoa has both the watershed and marine ecosystem expertise to address this issue at present. However, existing data collected by different resource agencies in American Samoa was combined to obtain a correlation between indicators of watershed and coral reef condition. The results of this initial study can help stimulate and guide new collaborative investigations of how watersheds and fishing are influencing coral reefs in American Samoa.

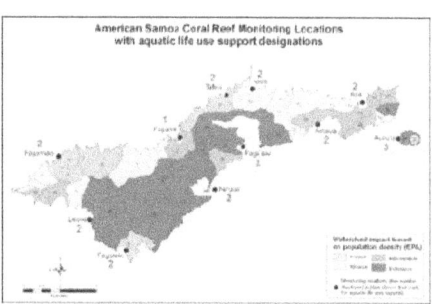

American Samoa Coral Reef Monitoring Locations with aquatic life use support designations

Key Partners and Information Sources

American Samoa Environmental Protection Agency, American Samoa Department of Marine and Wildlife Resources, American Samoa Department of Commerce.

Results and Decision Support Products

- Compared to other sites in American Samoa, Fagatele Bay NMS ranks high in coral cover and high in fish species richness.
- Fagatele Bay has relatively few large fish and thus ranks low in fish biomass.
- Coral cover, fish species richness and fish biomass show no statistical relationship to watershed area and human population density adjacent to the sites studied.
- Factors other than those related to human population in watersheds are controlling coral and fish populations.
- Data are needed on the intensity of fishing pressure at the different study sites, as well as runoff rates into coastal areas adjacent to the different watersheds.

Management Response

This simple mining of existing data within different American Samoa Government Agencies shows the need to build collaborative, multi-agency programs to better understand the drivers of coral reef condition in American Samoa. This may best be achieved though the Coral Reef Advisory Group (CRAG), whose members include all the AS Government agencies with marine resource management efforts. An Interagency Cooperative Agreement has been drafted to formalize better collaboration and is under review by the CRAG partners. However, the informal collaborations built by Fagatele Bay NMS science and education staff have already been successful in enhancing awareness of local agency resources, showing how these resources can be used to address marine management issues and creating wider understanding of the condition of American Samoa's marine environment.

NATIONAL MARINE SANCTUARIES

Florida Keys National Marine Sanctuary

Management Issue

Designing the Tortugas Ecological Reserve

Implementation of marine reserves in the U.S. is a contentious environmental issue because of the deeply rooted tradition of treating the oceans as a commons to be exploited with impunity. As an ocean conservation ethic evolves in the U.S. and as natural resources become more scarce, there is greater acceptance of marine reserves as a legitimate approach to conservation. However, there are currently few fully protected marine reserves in the U.S. that can be used as examples of success, either because they have not been implemented long enough to show positive benefits or they are poorly designed and managed. The Tortugas 2000 Working Group reviewed available scientific and socioeconomic information and made a recommendation to NOAA on the size, shape, and placement of the Tortugas Ecological Reserve.

Information Needs

- A site characterization for the Tortugas region, focusing on oceanography, benthic habitats, and fisheries
- Geographic Information Systems (GIS) based data sets that integrate biological and human-use information
- Public and Working Group input on and responses to scientific information on ecological and socioeconomic aspects of the area

Scientific Approach and Actions

- Scientific literature review and expert consultation: White papers commissioned by NOAA and the National Park Service to provide the Working Group and other interested parties with up-to-date information on oceanography, fish and fisheries, spatial extent of natural resources (e.g., deepwater coral banks), and connectivity of Tortugas area to broader region.

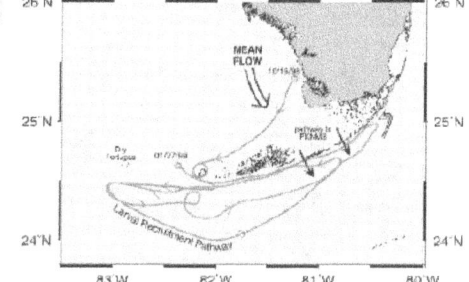

- Map resources and uses at a fine scale (1 sq. nautical mile) to facilitate decision-making.
- Synthesize existing scientific information and traditional knowledge
- Convene multi-stakeholder working group, including scientists, to draft boundary alternatives based on best available information

Key Partners and Information Sources

National Park Service, Rosenstiel School of Marine and Atmospheric Science (Univ. of Miami), Pfleger Institute of Environmental Research, Environmental Defense, NOAA National Marine Fisheries Service, NOAA Atlantic Oceanographic and Meteorological Laboratory, Chief Economist of the National Marine Sanctuary Program, NOAA National Undersea Research Center-Univ. of North Carolina at Wilmington, recreational and commercial users.

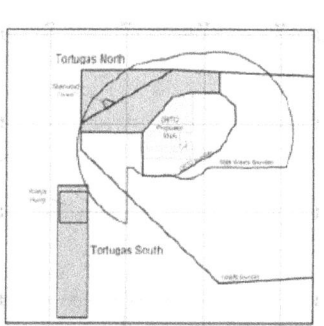

Results and Decision Support Products

- GIS mapping tool to evaluate different boundary scenarios
- Maps of oceanic circulation, potential larval retention regions, benthic habitats, biological resources, and human uses
- Location of a regionally significant reef fish spawning aggregation sites

Management Response

The Florida Keys NMS convened two informational forums to: (1) present to the Working Group and others the best-available scientific information on ecological and socioeconomic aspects of the area, (2) allow community members to share their knowledge of and experience in the Tortugas region, and (3) inform the Working Group about uses of the area. The Working Group's consensus agreement on a recommended preferred alternative set the stage for the many approvals required from the seven state and federal agencies that had oversight over the implementation of different jurisdictional components of the Tortugas Ecological Reserve; full implementation occurred on July 1, 2001 of the two areas (Tortugas North and South) that comprise the reserve.

Information from: Cowie-Haskell, B.D., and J.M. Delaney. 2003. Integrating science into the design of the Tortugas Ecological Reserve. Mar. Technol. Soc. J. 37. 68-79. http://floridakeys.noaa.gov/tortugas/welcome.html

Florida Keys National Marine Sanctuary

Management Issue:

Effectiveness of a Marine Reserve: Spiny Lobster

Spiny lobsters support one of Florida's most economically important commercial fisheries and a large recreational fishery. Historically, spiny lobsters were not considered good candidates for protection in reserves because of their migratory nature. Studies in the Florida Keys have found that, depending upon their location and size, reserves may protect juveniles until they mature and enter the fishery, and protect or enhance existing spawning stock.

Information Needs

- Whether the size and shape of the reserve relative to the home range of spiny lobster and the location of key habitats is sufficient for protection
- Whether the spawning potential of spiny lobsters is increasing through increasing abundance and/or size within the reserve relative to an adjacent fished area

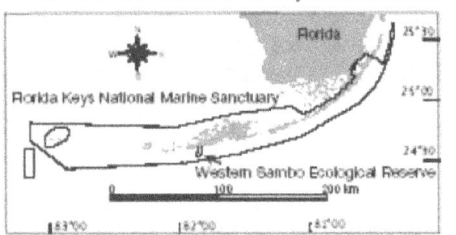

Scientific Approach and Actions

Field observations and measurements collected within the Western Sambo Ecological Reserve and at Pelican Shoal (fished)

Key Partners and Information Sources

Florida Fish and Wildlife Conservation Commission, Fish and Wildlife Research Institute

Results and Decision Support Products

- Reports to FKNMS staff
- Presentation to the Sanctuary Advisory Council
- Publication in a peer-reviewed scientific journal

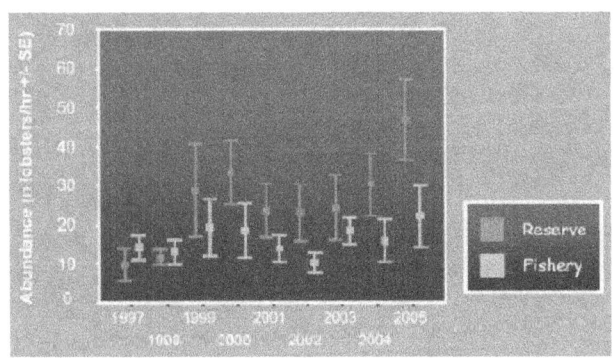

Management Response

Sanctuary managers, the Sanctuary Advisory Council, and the public have data showing the build-up in abundance (top panel) and size (bottom panel) in the Western Sambo Ecological Reserve relative to Pelican Shoal (open to the lobster fishery). These data support a success with respect to one of the primary purposes of the ecological reserve – to protect ecosystem function, in this case by restoring the ecological role of spiny lobster to a more natural, unfished condition. The studies are part of a longer term approach to evaluate effectiveness of reserves of differing sizes and shapes for different resources throughout the Florida Keys and elsewhere in the system of marine sanctuaries.

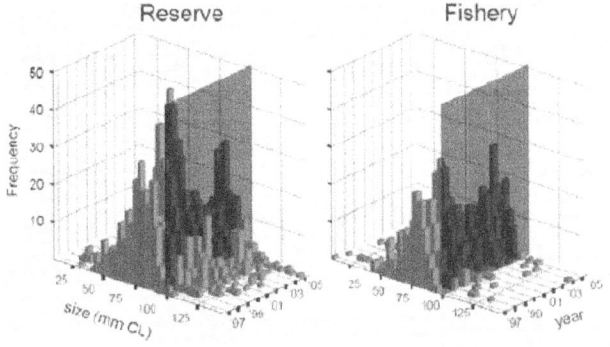

Florida Keys National Marine Sanctuary

Management Issue

Emergency Response Planning in the Florida Keys

NOAA's National Marine Sanctuaries Program and Office of Response and Restoration, in partnership with the U.S. Coast Guard, the State of Florida, and others, conducted an emergency response exercise in the Florida Keys NMS in April 2005. Called Safe Sanctuaries 2005, the exercise was different from most response drills as it was driven primarily by NOAA trustee and emergency response mandates. The exercise highlighted NOAA's science, including the ability to deliver data, observations, forecasts, and expertise during emergencies threatening life, commerce, and the environment. Experience and training gained is being applied in other sanctuaries and NOAA-wide to enhance efficiency and effectiveness of response actions.

Information Needs

- High resolution bathymetric charts to identify details of coral reef habitat and sunken historical resources.
- Ocean and meteorological observation systems to measure operating conditions in real-time.
- Integrating ocean/atmospheric observations with models to support multi-agency emergency response decisions.
- Ground truth surveys to validate models and determine potential injury to benthic habitats, shoreline communities and historic resources.

Scientific Approach and Actions

Scientific literature reviews and expert meetings were conducted to evaluate response actions. Computer simulation models were combined with real-time observing systems to forecast weather and pollution transport. Model forecast were validated with field observation using drift cards to simulate pollution transport. Geo-databases (SHIELDS/RUST) were populated and queried to identify potential pollution sources, sensitive resources, and to track response strategies. Bathymetric surveys were conducted with data processing completed at sea and transmitted to the command post in real time.

Key Partners and Information Sources

U.S. Coast Guard, Florida Department of Environmental Protection, Florida Fish and Wildlife Conservation Service, Monroe County, National Park Service, Titan Maritime Industries, Inc., Clean Caribbean Americas, Genwest Systems, Inc., NOAA Ocean Service, NOAA Weather Service, NOAA Environmental Satellite Service, NOAA Research, NOAA National Marine Fisheries Service, NOAA Marine and Aviation Operations, NOAA Office of Public, Constituent and Intergovernmental Affairs, NOAA Office of Legislative Affairs.

Results and Decision Support Products

- High resolution charts delineating vessel salvage and resource impacts.
- Maps of biological communities and maritime heritage sites recommended for protection.
- Real-time current, weather, and pollution forecasts.
- Sanctuaries Hazardous Incident Emergency Logistics Database System (SHIELDS) and Resources and Under Sea Threats (RUST) information systems.
- Field survey data from shoreline and coral reef areas.

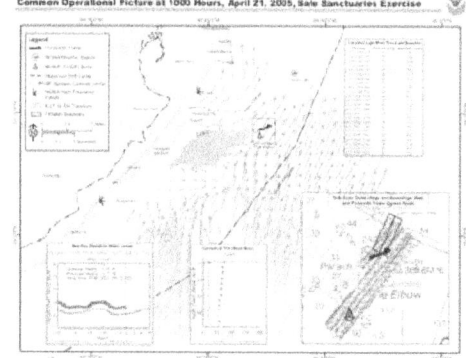

Management Response

During the response, a multi-agency unified command (Federal, State, and private) identified response options for oil spills in especially sensitive habitats, interagency operating protocols, and new applications of NOAA real-time data and products. Information gained is being incorporated into local area response plans. NOAA programs are updating operational plans, including safety training, internal communications, and agency-wide concept of operations.

Florida Keys National Marine Sanctuary

Restoration Tools for Injured Seagrass Communities

Seagrass communities are key to healthy ecosystems in the Florida Keys NMS. Seagrass habitat is frequently destroyed by human activities such as vessel groundings and dredging. NOAA's response to incidents damaging seagrass includes injury assessment, restoration, and monitoring, each of which requires understanding of natural dynamics of seagrasses and their habitats and patterns of natural recovery. Case settlement and litigation require data to support economic assessments that determine the value of lost resource services between the time of injury and the time of full recovery.

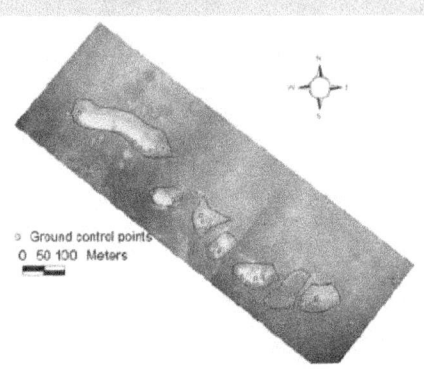

Grounding sites (exposed sand) in seagrass meadows.

Information Needs

- Seagrass recovery rates under various environmental conditions, differing levels of injury severity, and using various techniques for recovery enhancement (infilling, transplantation, and fertilization by attracting seabirds using perches).
- Models of recovery to support Habitat Equivalency Analysis (HEA)

Scientific Approach and Actions

Empirical assessments of rates of recolonization and lateral growth using in-water and aerial data; literature reviews to support modeling and HEA; post-restoration monitoring of restored sites.

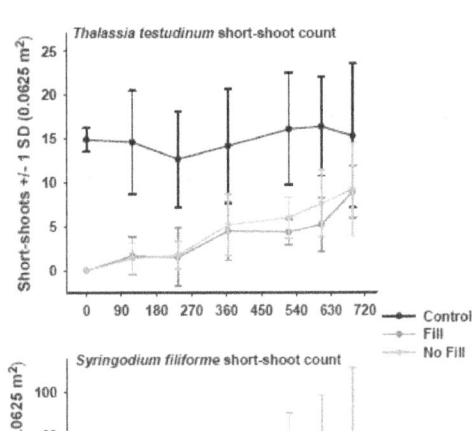

Key Partners and Information Sources

NOAA National Centers for Coastal Ocean Science; NOAA Damage Assessment Center; NOAA General Council for Natural Resources; Florida Fish and Wildlife Conservation Commission; Fish and Wildlife Research Institute

Results and Decision Support Products

- Multiple peer reviewed journal publications on seagrass recovery by Kenworthy and others
- ARC GIS and statistical spatial models by Fonseca and others
- HEA-support recovery model and Mini-312 program by Kirsch and others

Management Response

Seagrass restoration studies have led to dramatically improved techniques that reduce collateral damage caused by the offending action, mitigate further degradation of injury sites, and enhance recovery rates beyond those that would occur naturally. Recovery models are used in all seagrass cases that require physical restoration, have been successfully employed during litigation in the prosecution of physical injury cases, and have enabled recovery of damages in accordance with model projections. Efforts are underway to modify and apply these tools to injuries in coral and rocky intertidal habitats.

Seabird on fertilization station.

Flower Garden Banks National Marine Sanctuary

Management Issue

Dispersant Use for Oil Spill Response

The Flower Garden Banks NMS helped develop a regional response plan for spills, part of which was consideration of "pre-approval" for the use of dispersants within and near the sanctuary, a change to pre-existing guidance, which excluded its use over the banks. Allowing dispersant use in order to promote dilution and microbial degradation, even under appropriate conditions, would move oil from the surface into the water column, and potentially to the bottom, either of which could put sanctuary resources at greater risk than leaving the oil on the surface and recovering it using other means (booms and skimmers, for example).

Information Needs

- Dispersal characteristics of oil with and without dispersants under varying oceanographic and meteorological conditions (e.g., concentration by depth)
- Toxicity test results for dispersed oil and dispersants for eggs, larvae and adults, especially for species indigenous to the Gulf or Mexico and similar to those found at the Flower Gardens
- Data on the effectiveness of impact minimization efforts in offshore environments (surface oil removal efficiency, dilution and degradation rates)

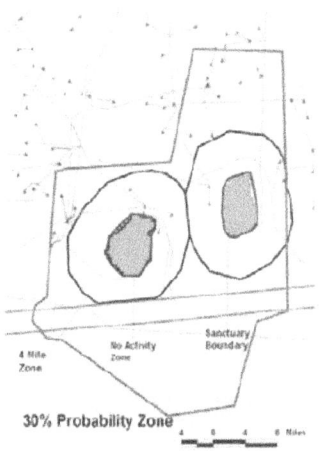

30% Probability Zone

Scientific Approach and Actions

Scientific literature review and expert consultation
Field observations and measurements made during test application during Mega Borg oil spill (1990)
Spill risk assessments (i.e. projected movement rates) using local oceanographic and meteorological data

Key Partners and Information Sources

Regional Response Team, NOAA Hazmat, Environmental Protection Agency, Minerals Management Service, National Ocean Industries Association, National Research Council, Geochemical and Environmental Research Group, Texas A&M University

Decision Support Products

- Sanctuary risk contour maps for 1-day, 3-day, and 10-day spill movement, based on projected trajectories using data on seasonal winds and currents
- Recommendation memo for NOAA representative to Regional Response Team

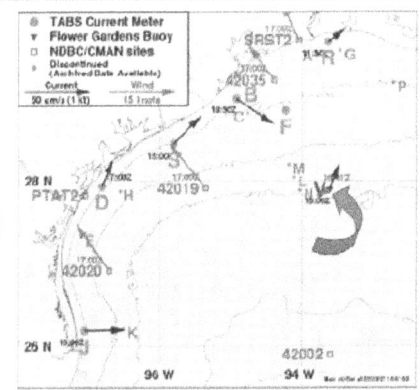

Management Response

Policy revision by NOAA in 1994 to facilitate dispersant use in the event that the Federal On-Scene Coordinator deems it appropriate, requesting application as far as possible from the sanctuary, avoiding use during certain key timeframes (e.g. seasonal species gatherings), consulting sanctuary management, and forwarding incident related data afterward.

NATIONAL MARINE
SANCTUARIES

Flower Garden Banks National Marine Sanctuary

Management Issue

Habitat Protection in the Northwestern Gulf of Mexico

Some of the undersea banks in the northwestern Gulf of Mexico are inadequately protected from certain human impacts, such as habitat destruction caused by vessel anchoring, treasure salvage, and destructive fishing techniques (e.g. bottom-tending trawls and longlines). The Flower Garden Banks NMS provided boundary recommendations to the Gulf of Mexico Fisheries Management Council for consideration as designated Habitat Areas of Particular Concern (HAPC) and Coral Habitats for numerous banks in the northwestern Gulf of Mexico.

Information Needs

- High resolution bathymetric charts to identify detail of Essential Fish Habitat and other particularly sensitive habitat types
- Groundtruthing surveys to determine benthic habitat characteristics, communities, and associated fish populations

Scientific Approach and Actions

Scientific literature review of historic investigations led to the acquisition of approximately 4000 sq. km of high resolution multibeam bathymetry of reefs and banks in the northwestern Gulf of Mexico. Groundtruthing cruises resulted in 175 Remotely Operated Vehicle (ROV) surveys, collection of 250 samples, and the collection of 8500 high resolution digital images. A searchable spatial database was produced during analysis of the images. The database inventories all biological components identified in the images.

Deep-water assemblage commonly found on banks of the northwestern Gulf of Mexico

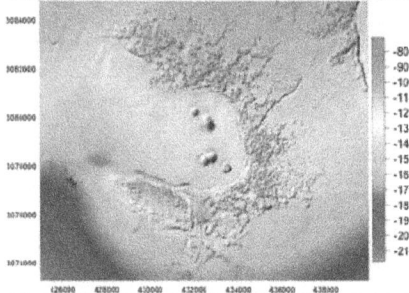

High resolution image of submerged features on the outer continental shelf (depth in meters) (USGS)

Key Partners and Information Sources

U.S. Geological Survey, University of New Hampshire, NOAA's Office of Ocean Exploration, Minerals Management Service, NOAA National Marine Fisheries Service, Gulf of Mexico Fisheries Management Council.

Results and Decision Support Products

- Habitat characterizations produced for several banks to identify areas recommended for protection
- High resolution multibeam charts, delineating boundary recommendations
- Images of biological communities recommended for protection

Management Response

The Gulf of Mexico Fisheries Management Council has recommended to NOAA National Marine Fisheries Service the designation of Habitat Areas of Particular Concern and Coral Habitats in the northwestern Gulf of Mexico based on boundary recommendations provided by the Flower Garden Banks National Marine Sanctuary. These designations will result in critical protections for these sensitive and unique habitats.

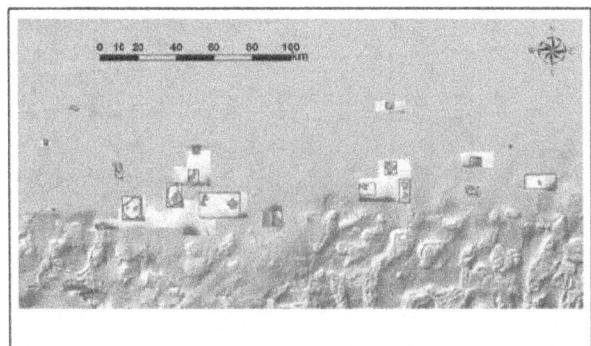

HAPC boundary recommendations provided to the Gulf of Mexico Fisheries Management Council

Gray's Reef National Marine Sanctuary

Habitat Map and Public Process Used to Guide Development of a Marine Research Area Concept

Information on the status and natural variability of resource components, species, and systems is essential for the informed management and is necessary to adequately differentiate between human-induced and natural change. Important research questions at Gray's Reef National Marine Sanctuary, including those related to human impacts on bottom-dwelling living resources, can only be addressed by studying an area in which these activities can be controlled. The concept of a Research Area was developed through comments obtained in public scoping for the Gray's Reef Draft Management Plan, resource and research workshops, and a recommendation from the Gray's Reef Sanctuary Advisory Council. The concept was further developed by convening a consensus-driven workshop comprised of constituents and experts. The group applied a science-based analytical tool to determine potential placement and size of such an area.

Information Needs

- Information on the bathymetry (bottom topography) of the site by collection of multibeam bathymetry
- Position and geographically referenced information relative to the location and size of persistent bottom features (e.g. ledges) which are important to key species in Gray's Reef collected by side-scanning sonar
- Spatial data of sites that are frequented by recreational fishermen in order to minimize their displacement
- Geo-referenced information related to sites in the sanctuary that have been used historically for research

Scientific Approach and Actions

A working group composed of sanctuary users, scientists, law enforcement, regional planners, educators and sanctuary staff was convened. The "Research Area Working Group" (RAWG) utilized a facilitated, consensus-driven process where issues, considerations, and concerns on potential placement and size of a research area were discussed at length by all participants. Placement prioritizations were determined by consensus and comments were recorded. Habitat maps that had been developed from data collected by multibeam and side-scanning sonar and ground-truthed by divers and towed video were used to develop a GIS-based analysis tool to maximize the number of high quality ledges, include the most number of previous research sites and minimize the displacement of recreational fishermen.

Key Partners and Information Sources

NOAA National Centers for Coastal Ocean Science, Regional planners, South Atlantic Fisheries Management Council (SAFMC), Georgia Department of Natural Resources, College of Charleston, Coastal Conservation Association (CCA), Reef Environmental Education Foundation (REEF), South Carolina Department of Natural Resources.

Results and Decision Support Products

- A GIS based Research Area analysis tool that was used to contribute to consensus-driven efforts to define a research area and which can be used for the public processes as the concept moves forward.
- Recommendations to both the Sanctuary Advisory Council (SAC) and to management of Gray's Reef NMS.

Management Response

Recommendations made by the RAWG were adopted in total by the SAC and were further recommended to Gray's Reef management. Gray's Reef management will additionally consider the implications, placement and implementation of a Research Area and take the concept to the next step of public involvement according to the National Environmental Policy Act (NEPA).

Gulf of the Farallones National Marine Sanctuary

Management Issue

Reduction of Chronic Oil Pollution: Clean up of the Sunken Vessel, S.S. *Jacob Luckenbach*

On July 14, 1953, the freighter *S.S. Jacob Luckenbach* collided with another vessel and sank in the Gulf of the Farallones NMS. As it decayed on the ocean floor, it leaked oil and became the source of many oil spills, primarily during large winter storms that rocked the vessel. The spills manifested in the appearance of tarballs and thousands of oiled seabirds on beaches from Bodega Bay to Monterey Bay. Major oiling events have occurred every few winters since at least 1973-74. It was not until January 2002 that these "mystery spills" were linked to the *Luckenbach*. Oil chemistry analysis confirmed the presence of *Luckenbach* oil on most of the tarballs and dead birds for every winter since 1992-93 (the earliest date for which samples are available).

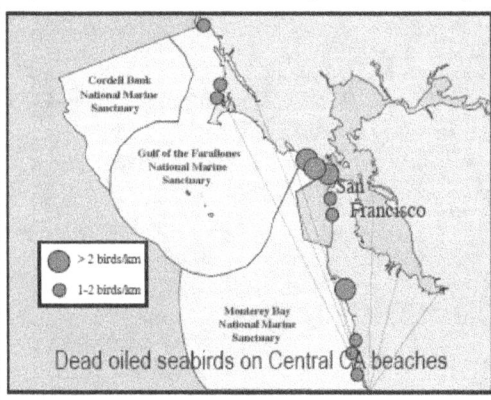

> 2 birds/km
1-2 birds/km

Dead oiled seabirds on Central CA beaches

Information Needs
- Historic and current rates of oiled seabirds, especially for Endangered and Threatened species
- Distribution, seasonal and annual patterns of oil pollution in the Gulf of the Farallones region
- Sources of oil pollution in the Gulf of the Farallones region

Scientific Approach and Actions
Long-term monitoring and sampling of tarballs, oiled seabirds and unoiled seabirds; laboratory analyses of archived, historic and current oil samples; identification and location of non-point sources and point sources of oil pollution.

Key Partners and Information Sources
NOAA Office of Response and Restoration, California Office of Spill Prevention and Response, Oil Chemistry Lab, NOAA Scientific Support Coordinator, Regional Response Team, Ford Ecological Consulting, Inc., US Coast Guard Marine Safety Office

Decision Support Products
- NOAA 2006 (S.S. *Jacob Luckenbach* and Associated Oil Spills: DARP)
- Roletto et al. 2003 & Hampton et al. 2003
- Resources & Undersea Threats (RUST) database
- NOAA Oil Spill Trajectory Model

Management Response
Trajectory hindcasts based on beached bird modeling were generated, and Fred Gamble and Robert Schwemmer's U.S. Pacific Coast Shipwreck Database were consulted to locate the *Luckenbach*. Subsequent removal of approximately 80% of the sunken oil (100% of the accessible oil) has resulted in a decline of oiled wildlife by more than 80%, based on seabird and shoreline monitoring programs developed to detect mortality events caused by natural and anthropogenic events, such as oil spills. Trained volunteers conduct emergency wildlife surveys and damage assessment data collection. Restoration activities are underway to return seabird population to historic levels.

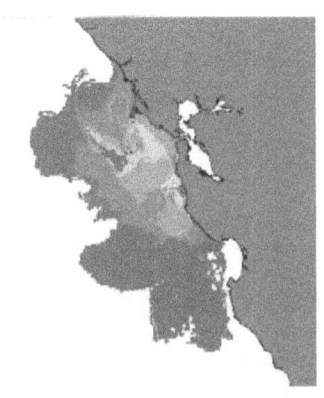

Gulf of the Farallones National Marine Sanctuary

Management Issue

Wildlife Disturbance and Recreational Use Conflicts

In the early 1990's, harbor seals in Tomales Bay experienced the highest level of disturbance of all haul out sites studied along the central California coast. Seals were disturbed during 49% of the surveys in 1983, and almost 100% of the time in 1992. Local constituents and resource managers were concerned about the number of disturbances to the seals, the low survival of harbor seal pups, and potential site abandonment. It was suspected that clam diggers near the haul out sites were the major source of disturbance. The sanctuary sought to minimize wildlife disturbance, while preserving recreational activities and traditional harbor seal haul outs.

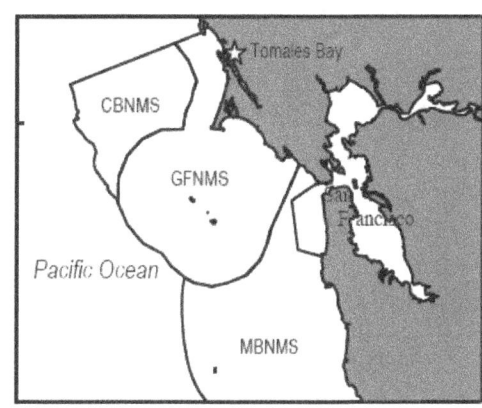

Information Needs

- Data on the sources of anthropogenic and natural disturbance to the seals.
- Data on the level of impacts, distance and duration of various human activities in relation to seal activities.
- Data on the effectiveness of docent and stewardship programs aimed at educating recreationists on compatible activities and wildlife viewing etiquette near seal haul out sites.

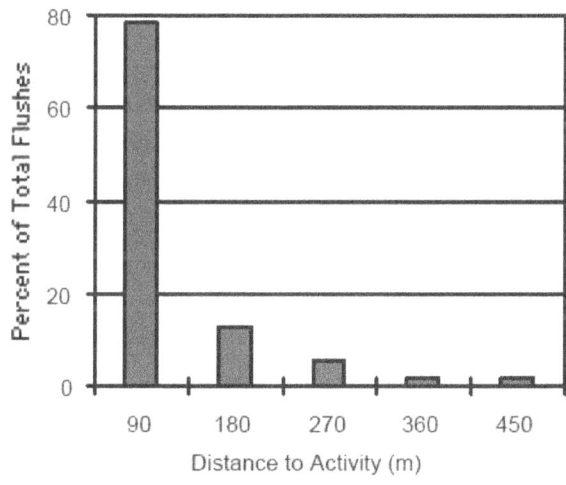

Scientific Approach and Actions

Scientific literature review and expert consultation on historic uses of haul out sites by humans and seals; field counts and behavior observations; measurements of human activities, distance to seals, seal behaviors, and pupping rates; measurements of changes caused by humans and reduction of disturbance levels after initiation of docent and stewardship programs.

Key Partners and Information Sources

Point Reyes National Seashore
National Park Service
National Marine Fisheries Service
Allen and King, 1992
Mortenson, 1996

Results and Decision Support Products

- Reports were produced and monitoring results were evaluated on behavior, haul out patterns and harbor seal populations within the Gulf of the Farallones National Marine Sanctuary.
- Community outreach and Interpretation programs were evaluated (including brochures, wildlife viewing guidelines and docent programs).
- Data library for use by NOAA General Council on human activities and correlated impacts.

Management Response

A wildlife interpretation program has been developed and implemented, and uses docents to teach the public about the presence and sensitivity of seals to human activities. Clam diggers continue to be the most frequent human activity on the Tomales Bay mudflats but now cause less than one percent of the disturbances to seals. Recreationists and wildlife now coexist and monitoring has shown that the survival rate of harbor seal pup has increased.

Hawaiian Islands Humpback Whale

Management Issue

Vessels colliding with whales

The sanctuary was concerned that an increasing humpback whale population, combined with vessel traffic in the sanctuary, would lead to an increased risk of serious or fatal vessel—whale collisions. This concern was born out of an increasing perception worldwide that vessel strikes could have serious impacts on the recovery of some endangered large whales.

Information Needs

- Review of NOAA National Marine Fisheries Service collision and stranding reports, and all relevant newspaper articles
- Synthesis and analysis for trends

Scientific Approach and Actions

The Sanctuary contracted University of Hawaii researchers to review all relevant materials, analyze for evidence of trends, and make recommendations.

- Report found increasing trend in collisions
- Report recommended Vessel-whale collision workshop

Key Partners and Information Sources

Sanctuary Advisory Council, University of Hawaii, and the State of Hawaii, Department of Land and Natural Resources, NOAA Fisheries stranding database and Hawaii newspaper archives.

Decision Support Products

- Sanctuary Advisory Council convened a workshop with experts (whale biologists, engineers and industry representatives) from across the country.
- Vessel- whale collision workshop made several recommendations prioritizing education and outreach in the short term and continued investigation of collision avoidance technologies for the future.
- Sanctuary Advisory Council recommended boater outreach program.
- Sanctuary Advisory Council also advised investigation of an anonymous reporting system.

Management Response

The sanctuary designed and produced a variety of materials and outreach initiatives to deliver messages to Hawaii boaters Highlights include:

- Strategically placed signage at harbors and boat ramps
- Press releases and media follow up generating extensive print and TV coverage
- Working with proposed high speed ferry company to develop an avoidance plan based on known whale distribution, behavior and environmental conditions, as well as proper watch-keeping

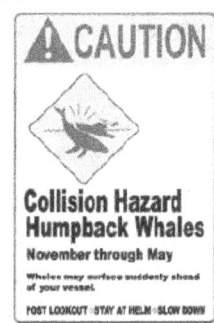

Monterey Bay National Marine Sanctuary

Management Issue

Beach COMBERS Inform Fishery Managers on Gillnet Bycatch

The Monterey Bay National Marine Sanctuary (MBNMS) consists of 5,322 square miles of ocean, and monitoring all aspects of the sanctuary is impossible. Because marine birds and mammals are top predators, their health can be used as an indicator of the quality and quantity of prey resources such as krill, squid and fishes. Using top predators as indicators of events such as El Niño, harmful algal blooms, oil spills and fishery impacts, is also convenient because the public values these animals and understands the need to study, protect, and conserve them and their habitats.

Information Needs

- Monitoring information on beachcast marine birds and mammals as an index of ecosystem health in the Monterey Bay National Marine Sanctuary
- Baseline information to demonstrate effects resulting from catastrophic events such as oil spills
- A consistent data set over long period of time to resolve subtle changes in environmental quality, which may not be apparent with short-term sampling
- Causes of seabird and marine mammal mortality
- Monitoring abundance of tar balls (oil patches) on beaches to determine pollution sources

Scientific Approach and Actions

In 1997, we initiated a beach survey program called Beach COMBERS (Coastal Ocean Mammal and Bird Education and Research Surveys). Using over 80 trained citizen-volunteers, beachcast marine birds and mammals are surveyed monthly at selected beaches. Currently, volunteers survey 70 km of beaches in the Monterey Bay National Marine Sanctuary as part of a network of interacting citizens, scientists, and resource managers.

Key Partners and Information Sources

Beach COMBERS volunteers, the Monterey Bay National Marine Sanctuary Integrated Monitoring Network (SIMoN), Moss Landing Marine Laboratories, California Department of Fish and Game's Marine Wildlife Veterinary Care and Research Center, NOAA National Marine Fisheries Service, and U.S. Fish and Wildlife Service

Results and Decision Support Products

- Nine years of consistent monthly surveys describing trends in the distribution and abundance of beachcast marine birds and mammals
- Reports on episodic mortality events related to natural (e.g., El Niño, harmful algal blooms) and anthropogenic (e.g., oil spills, fishery bycatch) factors
- A comprehensive website for volunteer support and reporting (http://www.mbnms-simon.org/sections/beachCombers/index.php?l=n)

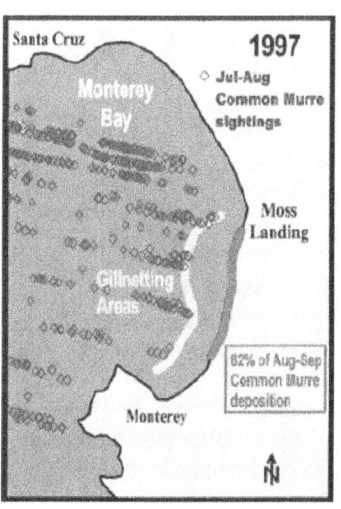

Management Response

Because of the increased deposition of Common Murres and porpoises reported by Beach COMBERS, which coincided with a nearshore gillnet fishery to catch halibut, NOAA National Marine Fisheries Service re-established an observer program for the California halibut gillnet fishery. In 2000, the California Department of Fish and Game changed fishing regulations to limit gillnets to water deeper than 360 feet to reduce bycatch mortality. Annually, thousands of seabirds and dozens of mammals now avoid bycatch in the Monterey Bay.

Information from SIMoN Action Plan
Beach COMBERS- http://www.mbnms-simon.org/sections/beachCombers/index.php?l=n
http://montereybay.noaa.gov/

NATIONAL MARINE SANCTUARIES

Monterey Bay National Marine Sanctuary

Management Issue

Characterize and Protect Davidson Seamount Habitat and Communities

Less than 0.1 percent of the world's seamounts have been explored to document the species that live on them. Many species found on seamounts that have been explored are new to science. The Monterey Bay National Marine Sanctuary (MBNMS) has led collaborative field surveys to explore and document communities at Davidson Seamount. These expeditions documented previously undiscovered species and assemblages including large patches of sponges and long-lived corals. There is currently no comprehensive management scheme in place to protect the organisms on the seamount or the surrounding ecosystem. In addition, there is a need for NOAA to educate the public about deep corals and seamounts.

Information Needs

- Taxonomic identification and natural history of rare or new species
- Age and growth determination of deep corals
- Distribution of deep coral and sponge communities
- Information for education programs on corals and seamounts

Scientific Approach and Actions

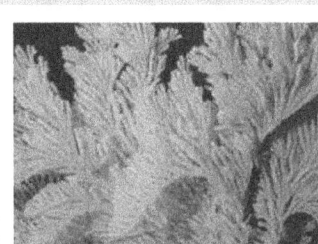

- Collect and preserve specimens, collect high-resolution images and video, and consult with knowledgeable scientists and specialized taxonomists
- Determine coral age and growth patterns using traditional sectioning techniques and novel radiometric ageing methods
- Develop and test a coral distribution model using bathymetric information, and current and particle measurement techniques
- Collect high-definition video for BBC's *Planet Earth* television series, and images for websites

Key Partners and Information Sources

Monterey Bay Aquarium Research Institute, Moss Landing Marine Laboratories, Monterey Bay Aquarium, NOAA National Marine Fisheries Service, fishermen, The Ocean Conservancy, World Wildlife Fund, NOAA's Office of Ocean Exploration, BBC

Results and Decision Support Products

- Annotated video (>150 hours), and high-resolution images (>200) catalogued in online photo database
- Age estimate for bamboo coral (*Keratoisis* sp.) exceed 200 years, and for precious coral (*Corallium* sp.) exceed 100 years
- Results published in 3 publications, 17 oral and 5 poster presentations, and award winning interactive CD ROM
- BBC's *Planet Earth* television series due in 2007

Management Response

- MBNMS presented Pacific Fishery Management Council (PFMC) with an opportunity to prepare draft Sanctuary regulations limiting fishing deeper than 3000 ft at Davidson Seamount
- PFMC endorsed goals and objectives of the sanctuary, requested protections be provided under Magnuson-Stevens Act, and identified protection of Davidson Seamount as one of the preferred alternatives for protection of essential groundfish habitat
- NOAA National Marine Fisheries Service will publish final rule in Spring 2006 prohibiting fishing deeper than 3000 ft at seamount
- Sanctuary Advisory Council proposed adding Davidson Seamount to MBNMS

Monterey Bay National Marine Sanctuary

Management Issue

Database Management for the Central and Northern California Ocean Observing System (CeNCOOS)

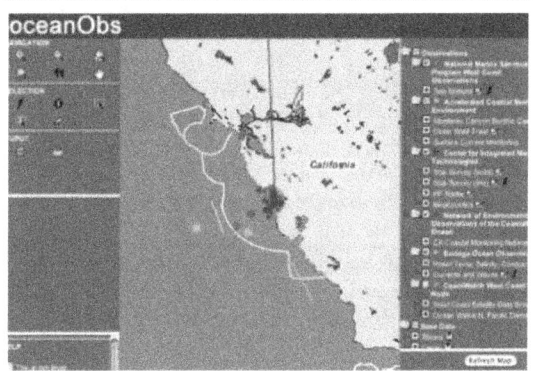

A top priority for NOAA is the development of an integrated ocean observing system (IOOS). Staff from NOAA's National Marine Sanctuaries Program have worked with coordinators of the Central and Northern California Ocean Observing System (CeNCOOS) to develop a database management system to inventory regional IOOS ocean observing activities. The system, called *oceanObs*, is a versatile, multi-use system that allows program managers to administer metadata on their activities, while providing a means for regional associations to query and report on programs in their region.

Information Needs

- Accurate reporting on ocean observing activities by coordinators of regional associations (RAs).
- Administration of observing information by individual observing programs.
- Public access to metadata and facilitation of observing data products discovery.

Scientific Approach and Actions

System requirements of *oceanObs* were gathered from CeNCOOS coordinators to ensure proper functionality. Database schema were developed from the already existing CeNCOOS geodatabase. The system was built out over the course of 8 months and was completed in August 2005. To date, metadata have been entered for 23 ocean observing programs in the CeNCOOS region. In March 2006 a dedicated administrative assistant joined CeNCOOS staff to enter metadata on all 55 observing programs in the region. This position, partially supervised by sanctuary staff, will result in the first complete, publicly accessible, inventory of observing program metadata in any IOOS region.

Key Partners and Information Sources

Central and Northern California Ocean Observing System; Monterey Bay National Marine Sanctuary's Sanctuary Integrated Monitoring Network (SIMoN); National Coastal Data Development Center (NCDDC); a wide variety of research institutions throughout Northern and Central California.

Results and Decision Support Products

- Inventory system that provides ocean observatory platform and sensor information, viewable in a spatial display.
- Database search engine that links data sets and synthesized data products in Central and Northern California.
- Report generation on observing activities (e.g., funding, IOOS variables) used by regional coordinators.
- Improved ability to plan deployment of additional observing instruments.

Management Response

oceanObs has been used extensively by the CeNCOOS coordinator to assess and report on observing activities in the Central and Northern California region. The system has also enabled managers at the Monterey Bay NMS to better understand regional ocean observing efforts and find overlaps with their resource management needs (e.g., ocean current models for spill response). *oceanObs* is being considered as a model for inventories of observing activities in other IOOS regions throughout the nation. Efforts are currently underway by the National Marine Sanctuary Program and the Coastal Services Center to assess *oceanObs'* suitability to manage the inventory needs of all IOOS regions.

Monterey Bay National Marine Sanctuary

Management Issue

Marine Protected Areas Decision Support Tool

Two multi-stakeholder processes are currently underway to evaluate marine protected areas (MPAs) on the Central California Coast, in state waters under the Marine Life Protection Act Initiative (MLPA), and in federal waters via a working group of the Monterey Bay National Marine Sanctuary (MBNMS). In addition, NOAA's Marine Protected Areas Center is interested in piloting approaches to gather and evaluate data relevant to regional MPA design efforts. An important component of these efforts is the development of a decision support tool that will aid the two working groups in evaluating spatial information and selecting alternative designs for MPA arrays in state and federal waters.

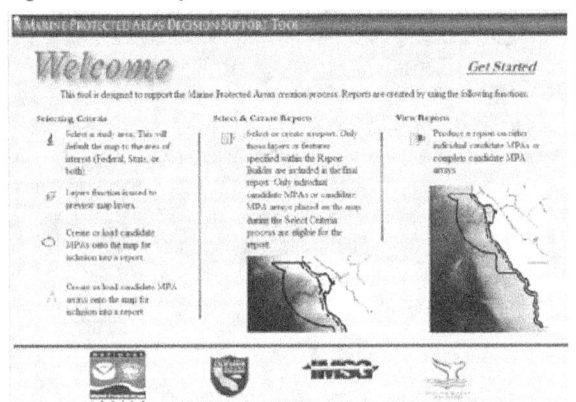

Information Needs

- Large volume and variety of spatial data (e.g., habitat, biological, oceanographic, consumptive and non-consumptive activities, regulatory boundaries, imagery and charts)
- Equal access "Decision support tool" for area analyses of proposed marine reserves

Scientific Approach and Actions

- Identify contractor to develop a common decision support tool for both the federal and state processes, and to allow future modifications as needed
- Guide tool development to include an interactive map for data exploration and visualization; provide for ease of use by all working group participants; and provide accurate area analyses of marine resources inside, outside, and across alternative marine reserve boundaries
- Coordinate with contractor and inter-agency GIS staff to populate decision support tool with spatial data

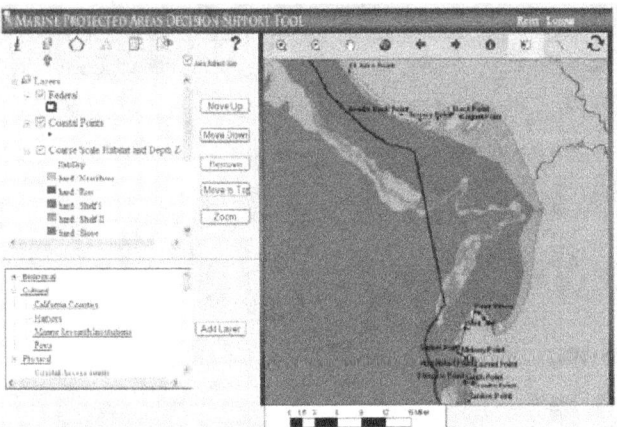

Key Partners and Information Sources

California Department of Fish and Game, National Marine Fisheries Service, Pacific Fisheries Management Council, I.M. Systems Group, Inc., MLPA and MBNMS Marine Protected Area working groups, fishing industry, University of California Santa Barbara, local research institutions and spatial data providers

Results and Decision Support Products

- Online interactive map and decision support tool developed
- Recommended boundary alternatives

Management Response

An extensive inter-agency collaborative effort has produced a powerful, web-based decision support tool. This convenient online tool allows all working group members to create their own individual marine reserve boundaries or even arrays of two or more reserves, while comparing and contrasting arrays published online by other working group members. Detailed reports summarize total area and relative percentage of federal and state marine resources inside, outside, and across individual marine reserves and any arrays they are nested within. Any computer with an Internet connection can access this tool, facilitating open and honest dialogue between all participants.

NATIONAL MARINE SANCTUARIES

For more information
http://sanctuaries.noaa.gov/jointplan/mb_mpa.html

Monterey Bay National Marine Sanctuary

Management Issue

Cruise Ship Discharges and Anchorage

Large cruise ships began visiting Monterey in 2002, and have increased their number of visits every year. These ships can provide local businesses with economic benefits, particularly if they introduce the region to tourists who may return for later visits. However, due to their sheer size, capacity for passengers, and environmental practices, cruise ships can cause serious impacts to the marine environment. Of main concern is the discharge of pollutants such as: sewage, also referred to as black water; gray water; oily bilge water; hazardous wastes and solid wastes. Cruise ships can also disturb the seafloor and alter habitat due to anchoring.

Information Needs
- Identify potential pollutants
- Determine optional discharge locations
- Assess southern Monterey Bay seafloor habitat types

Scientific Approach and Actions
- Collect information on all potential pollutants, including their potential impact on the environment
- Determine all U.S. regulations that govern discharge of pollutants and other materials
- Collect relevant spatial data (e.g., regulatory boundaries and habitat data)
- Identify critical habitats that anchorage should avoid
- Monitor all cruise ship discharges by building a spatial database of the sewage and gray water discharge record book (kept aboard every cruise ship)

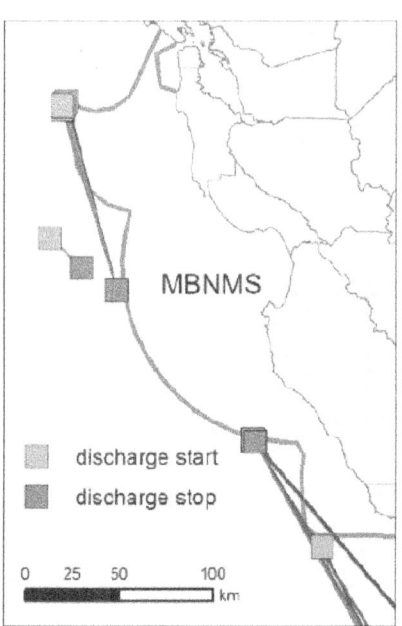

Key Partners and Information Sources
Cruise ship industry, City of Monterey, California State Water Resources Control Board, local Regional Water Quality Control Board, tourism industry

Results and Decision Support Products
- Initiated in 2004: monitoring of cruise ship discharge locations through a Geographic Information System (GIS)
- GIS database of all cruise ship discharge locations, regulatory boundaries, and seafloor data (e.g., habitat type, bathymetry, and complexity)

Management Response
All cruise ship discharges are mapped to verify agreements to avoid areas within the Sanctuary. Two anchorage points are designated to avoid sensitive kelp and rocky reef habitats. These responses will help reduce impacts to Monterey Bay National Marine Sanctuary resources from the presence of cruise ships.

Olympic Coast National Marine Sanctuary

Management Issue

Area to be Avoided (ATBA) Vessel Monitoring

A catastrophic discharge of oil from a maritime accident poses the single greatest risk to the Olympic Coast National Marine Sanctuary (OCNMS). OCNMS worked with the US Coast Guard and the International Maritime Organization to establish an Area to be Avoided (ATBA) as a buffer and allow assistance to adrift vessels along this rocky and environmentally sensitive coast. All ships transiting the area and carrying cargoes of oil or hazardous materials, and all ships 1,600 gross tons, are requested to avoid this area. The voluntary vessel routing measure, along with the seasonal positioning of a rescue tug in Neah Bay, has proven effective in preventing oil spills within the OCNMS. Sanctuary and vessel traffic mangers have a need to monitor the effectiveness of the ATBA and periodically make changes.

Information Needs

- Information on ATBA compliance.
- Position information on vessel transits.
- Information on vessel characteristics including; vessel name, vessel class, gross tonnage and in some cases cargo.
- Contact information for the ship's owners, operators or agents.
- Trend information on vessel behavior by class, tonnage, and ownership.

Scientific Approach and Actions

Since 1998 the sanctuary has acquired monthly vessel position files from the Canadian Coast Guard's radar site on Vancouver Island. This information is displayed as tracklines on a geographic information system. The data also includes vessel attributes that allows spatial and temporal analysis of behavior and trends, based on vessel characteristics.

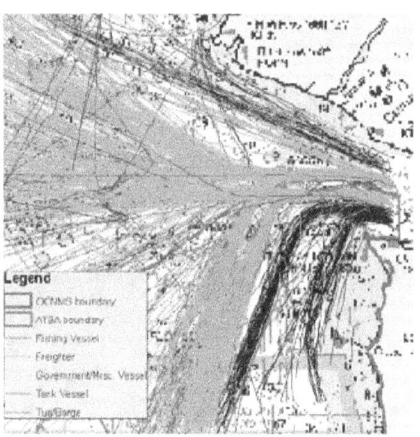

Key Partners and Information Sources

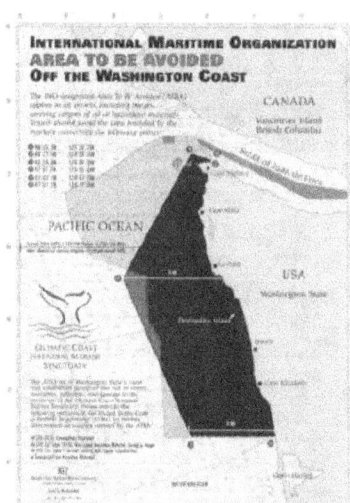

Vessel traffic in the northern section of OCNMS is jointly managed by the US and Canadian Coast Guards, under the Cooperative Vessel Traffic Service. The ATBA Vessel Monitoring and Outreach Program is supported by both these parties. The sanctuary receives vessel traffic data for post processing monthly from the Canadian Coast Guard along with limited real time access to vessel information from the US Coast Guard.

Results and Decision Support Products

- Monthly shape files of vessel transits.
- Monthly transit plots of non-complying vessels.
- Annual ATBA vessel compliance summaries.

Management Response

The monthly transit plots are used as part of an outreach effort to the marine industry. Letters are sent out under signature of the sanctuary superintendent and the Coast Guard captain of the port to vessels observed within the ATBA. The response by the maritime industry has been very favorable, with a 97% compliance rate in 2005.

Information from Olympic Coast National Marine Sanctuary Website. For more information.
http://olympiccoast.noaa.gov/protection/atba/welcome.html

Olympic Coast National Marine Sanctuary

Management Issue

Document and Protect Remaining Deep Coral/Sponge Communities

Deep coral and sponge communities in many parts of the ocean are threatened by potentially destructive human activities. The Olympic Coast National Marine Sanctuary (OCNMS) collaborated on a 2004 survey to document deep coral and sponge communities in the sanctuary. These discoveries included very rare species (e.g., *Lophelia pertusa*) and others that are very vulnerable to disturbance from bottom fishing gear. Remaining communities of these sensitive species need to be documented and options for long-term protection must be considered in order to avoid further impact and allow for recovery of impacted habitats.

Information Needs

- Current distribution of deep coral and sponge communities
- Areas with evidence of former existence of live communities
- Condition of existing communities (intact or damaged by fishing gear or other human activities)
- Relative risk of species composing the communities
- Relative distribution and intensity of potentially destructive human activities (principally fishing)

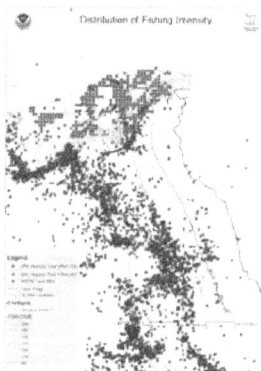

Scientific Approach and Actions

- Literature review and consultations with knowledgeable scientists and fishermen
- Acoustic mapping surveys (both side-scan sonar and multibeam bathymetry) to locate promising sites
- Video groundtruthing with remotely operated vehicles and collection of voucher specimens at target sites

Key Partners and Information Sources

NOAA National Centers for Coastal Ocean Science, NOAA National Marine Fisheries Service (NMFS), Washington Department of Fish and Wildlife, Pacific Fisheries Management Council (PFMC), coastal tribes, University of Washington, local fishermen

Results and Decision Support Products

- GIS-based data (bathymetric and topographic maps, groundtruthing locations)
- Results and unique species reports published in NOAA Technical Memorandum
- Poster presentation at Deep Sea Coral Symposium

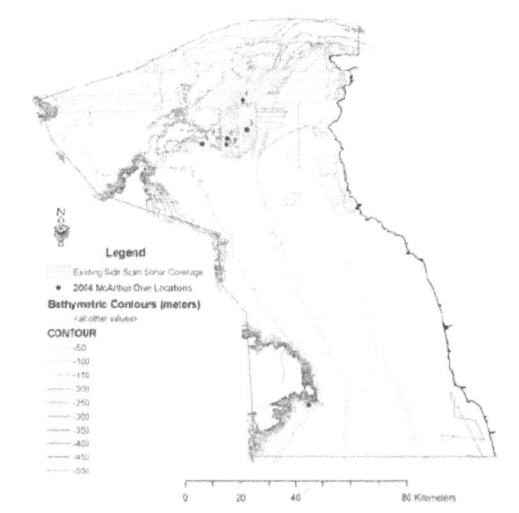

Management Response

OCNMS alerted NMFS and PFMC to the presence of coral/sponge areas in the sanctuary. PFMC/NMFS proposed protecting biogenic habitat areas, including some sites within OCNMS, as part of defining essential fish habitat for groundfish. Additional funding sources were secured for expanded surveys in 2006.

Stellwagen Bank National Marine Sanctuary

Rerouting Commercial Vessel Traffic to Reduce the Risk of Shipstrikes to Whales

The Stellwagen Bank NMS (SBNMS) has been working to mitigate the risk of shipstrikes to endangered whales. The sanctuary is a critical seasonal feeding area for right, humpback, fin, and minke whales. It is also the area in which large commercial ships converge to enter the Port of Boston. Over 200 large commercial ships ply the waters of the Stellwagen Bank NMS every month. The sanctuary, in cooperation with key partners, considered altering the traffic separation scheme in order to reduce shipstrikes in areas with high whale concentrations, as well as the economic impacts of such an action.

- Long-term distribution of baleen whale sightings
- Habitat characterization
- Whale feeding ecology
- Characterization of large commercial vessel use of SBNMS
- Requirements for proposal to International Maritime Organization

- Risk analysis of shipstrikes to whales using maps of whale sightings, habitats, human uses and information on whale feeding ecology

NOAA Office of Protected Resources, NOAA Northeast Fisheries Science Center, NOAA General Counsel for International Law, Right Whale Consortium, Massachusetts Port Authority, Shipping Industry, US Coast Guard, Whale Center of New England, Provincetown Center for Coastal Studies.

- An analysis of shipstrikes along the East Coast from 1979-2002 indicates that Massachusetts Bay, including the Stellwagen Bank NMS, is a hotspot for shipstrikes.
- The sanctuary is heavily used by large cargo vessels and by whales year around.
- A 23-year database of whale sightings reveal the existence of three areas of high whale density and that the current traffic safety separation bisects one of them.
- For vessels using the traffic separation scheme, rotating the scheme 12 degrees to the north may reduce risk of shipstrikes to endangered right whales by 58% and to all baleen whales by 81%.
- Vessel transit times would be increased by between 9 – 22 minutes

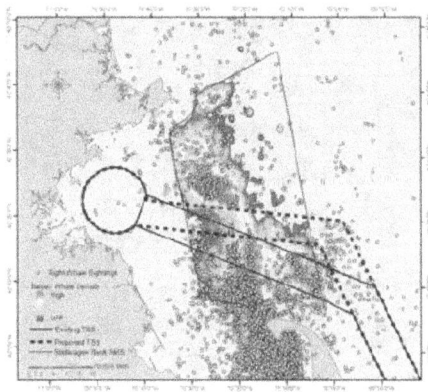

The National Marine Sanctuary Program, NOAA Office of Protected Resources, and the General Counsel for International Law have agreed to jointly propose to International Maritime Organization (IMO) to shift the current TSS 12 degrees to the north so that ships pass between two areas that have historically shown high densities of whales.

ACKNOWLEDGMENTS

I appreciate the efforts of those who prepared and reviewed material for this report: Ed Bowlby, Maria Brown, Erica Burton, Kathy Dalton, Andrew DeVogelaere, Bill Douros, Sarah Fangman, Ben Haskell, Patricia Hay, Emma Hickerson, Brian Keller, Bill Kiene, Chad King, Dani Lipski, Jean de Marignac, Dave Mattila, Greg McFall, Josh Pederson, Jan Roletto, George Schmahl, Natalie Senyk and David Wiley. They are also some of the people leading efforts in marine sanctuaries to conduct and facilitate science that supports resource management. I also want to recognize the many partners who conduct research in the sanctuaries.   Many of them are listed in the one page summaries under "Key Partners and Information Sources." For all these hard working people, we should all be grateful.

LITERATURE CITED

Allen, S.G. and M. E. King. 1992. Proceedings from the Third Biennial State of Tomales Bay Conference. Inverness CA, 1992, pp. 33-57

Cowie-Haskell, B.D., and J.M. Delaney. 2003. Integrating science into the design of the Tortugas Ecological Reserve. Mar. Technol. Soc. J. 37: 68-79.

Cox, C., and J.H. Hunt. 2005. Change in size and abundance of Caribbean spiny lobsters *Panulirus argus* in a marine reserve in the Florida Keys National Marine Sanctuary, USA. Mar. Ecol. Prog. Ser. 294: 227-239.

Hampton, S., R.G. Ford, H.R. Carter, C. Abraham, and D. Humple. 2003. Chronic oiling and seabird mortality from the sunken vessel S.S. Jacob Luckenbach in Central California. Marine Ornithology 31(1):35-41.

Mortenson, J. 1996. Human interference with harbor seals at Jenner, CA, 1994-1995. Unpublished report for Stewards of Slavianka Sonoma State Beaches, Russian River/Mendocino Park District, California Department of State Parks and Recreation. Duncan's Mills, CA. 48 pp.

National Centers for Coastal Ocean Science (NCCOS). 2005. A biogeographic assessment of the Channel Islands National Marine Sanctuary: A review of boundary expansion concepts for NOAA's. National Marine Sanctuary Program. NOAA Tech. Memorandum NOS NCCOS 21. 215 pp.

Luckenbach Trustee Council. 2006. S.S. Jacob Luckenbach and Associated Mystery Oil Spills Draft Damage Assessment and Restoration Plan/Environmental Assessment. Prepared by California Department of Fish and Game, National Oceanic and Atmospheric Administration, United States Fish and Wildlife Service, National Park Service. Sacramento, CA. 160 pp.

Roletto, J., J. Mortenson, I. Harrald, J. Hall, and L. Grella. 2003. Beached bird surveys and chronic oil pollution in Central California. Marine Ornithology 31(1): 21-28.

OTHER ONMS CONSERVATION SERIES PUBLICATIONS

The following reports have been published in the Marine Sanctuaries Conservation Series. All publications are available on the Office of National Marine Sanctuaries website (http://www.sanctuaries.noaa.gov/).

Normalization and characterization of multibeam backscatter: Koitlah Point to Point of the Arches, Olympic Coast National Marine Sanctuary - Survey HMPR-115-2004-03 (ONMS-06-03)

Developing Alternatives for Optimal Representation of Seafloor Habitats and Associated Communities in Stellwagen Bank National Marine Sanctuary (ONMS-06-02)

Benthic habitat mapping in the Olympic Coast National Marine Sanctuary (ONMS-06-01)

Channel Islands deep water monitoring plan development workshop report (ONMS-05-05)

Movement of yellowtail snapper (*Ocyurus chrysurus* Block 1790) and black grouper (*Mycteroperca bonaci* Poey 1860) in the northern Florida Keys National Marine Sanctuary as determined by acoustic telemetry (MSD-05-4)

The impacts of coastal protection structures in California's Monterey Bay National Marine Sanctuary (MSD-05-3)

An annotated bibliography of diet studies of fish of the southeast United States and Gray's Reef National Marine Sanctuary (MSD-05-2)

Noise levels and sources in the Stellwagen Bank National Marine Sanctuary and the St. Lawrence River Estuary (MSD-05-1)

Biogeographic analysis of the Tortugas Ecological Reserve (MSD-04-1)

A review of the ecological effectiveness of subtidal marine reserves in central California (MSD-04-2, MSD-04-3)

Pre-construction coral survey of the M/V *Wellwood* grounding site (MSD-03-1)

Olympic Coast National Marine Sanctuary: Proceedings of the 1998 Research Workshop, Seattle, Washington (MSD-01-04)

Workshop on Marine Mammal Research & Monitoring in the National Marine Sanctuaries (MSD-01-03)

A review of marine zones in the Monterey Bay National Marine Sanctuary (MSD-01-2)

Distribution and sighting frequency of reef fishes in the Florida Keys National Marine Sanctuary (MSD-01-1)

Flower Garden Banks National Marine Sanctuary: A rapid assessment of coral, fish, and algae using the AGRRA protocol (MSD-00-3)

The economic contribution of whalewatching to regional economies: Perspectives from two national marine sanctuaries (MSD-00-2)

Olympic Coast National Marine Sanctuary Area to be Avoided education and monitoring program (MSD-00-1)

Multi-species and multi-interest management: an ecosystem approach to market squid (*Loligo opalescens*) harvest in California (MSD-99-1)